Wolfgang Amadeus Mozart

MASS
in C minor

K 427

Vocal Score

Edited by

RICHARD MAUNDER

Music Department
OXFORD UNIVERSITY PRESS
Oxford and New York

Oxford University Press, Walton Street, Oxford OX2 6DP, England

Oxford University Press Inc., 198 Madison Avenue, New York, NY 10016, USA

Oxford is a trade mark of Oxford University Press

This edition is available in Germany, Austria, and Switzerland from
Carus-Verlag, Stuttgart (CV 40.630).

The full score is also on sale. Full scores, vocal scores, and instrumental
parts are available for hire from the publisher's hire library.
Scoring: S.S.T.B. soloists, S.A.T.B. double chorus, flute, 2 oboes, 2 bassoons, 2 horns,
2 trumpets, 3 trombones, timpani, strings, and continuo.

Duration: *c*.55 minutes

CONTENTS

INTRODUCTION

Shortly before Wolfgang Amadeus Mozart married Constanze Weber on 4 August 1782 he vowed that, in thanksgiving, he would write a large-scale setting of the mass. Five months later he reported to his father, Leopold, that it was already half finished:

It is quite true about my moral obligation; and I did not let that expression flow from my pen unintentionally. I truly made this promise to myself, and I truly hope to keep it. When I made it my wife was still single—but since I had firmly resolved to marry her soon after her convalescence, it was easy for me to make the promise. As you know, however, circumstances have frustrated our planned journey [to Salzburg]; but the score of half a mass, which is lying here in the best expectations, is the proof that I really made the promise. (4 January 1783)

It seems, therefore, that Mozart already had it in mind to perform the work in Salzburg, during the visit that he planned to make with Constanze to his father and sister. The visit had to be postponed to July 1783, and the performance took place in St Peter's, Salzburg, on 26 October, with Constanze singing the soprano solos.

At that time, however, Mozart had completed only the Kyrie, Gloria, Sanctus, 'Osanna', and Benedictus (though he had also drafted two movements, 'Credo in unum Deum' and 'Et incarnatus est', for the Credo, but had not fully orchestrated them), and only these completed movements were performed. The Mass was not repeated, and so Mozart never resumed work on it, although in March 1785 he arranged the Kyrie and Gloria as the Italian oratorio *Davidde penitente*, to new words possibly by Lorenzo da Ponte.

Unfortunately even Mozart's incomplete autograph has not survived intact, for all that remains of the Sanctus and 'Osanna' is the separate *particella* for wind and drums; the Benedictus is missing altogether. For these three movements the only other source (apart from the original trombone and organ parts) is a manuscript score made by Pater Matthäus Fischer (1763–1840) of Augsburg. Fischer's score was obviously made from a set of parts, and therefore was not copied directly from Mozart's autograph. Moreover he was a rather inaccurate copyist; and in the 'Qui tollis', Sanctus, and 'Osanna' he had to compress the eight vocal parts onto four staves in order to get the full score onto his manuscript paper. In the latter two movements he left his work incomplete, for only four parts (very occasionally five) are entered into his score.

There are, consequently, two separate problems to be faced in making a performing edition of the surviving material. First, the missing parts of the orchestration in the 'Credo in unum Deum' and 'Et incarnatus est' have to be completed, in the style of the rest of the Mass. There are two blank staves throughout Mozart's draft of the latter movement, almost certainly for two horns, so parts for those instruments have been added, with horn I joining the woodwind concertino from time to time.

Secondly, the Sanctus and 'Osanna' have to be reconstructed from Mozart's *particella* and Fischer's incomplete score. Fortunately the missing vocal parts in the 'Osanna' fugue are doubled by the orchestra most of the time, though Fischer's unsystematic way of working implies that the four parts in his copy do not necessarily represent the *same* four parts throughout. Freed from any such restrictive assumption, it is possible to reconstruct the fugue in a way that takes full account of Mozart's division of his voices into two separate four-part choirs, so that, for example, the subject and countersubject always appear together in the same choir.

It should be noted that no distinction is made in this vocal score between the original sources and editorial emendations and additions: for full details, see the full score, also published by Oxford University Press. Word division follows the autograph, and is consistent with the Austro–German pronunciation of the Latin text that Mozart would have expected.

RICHARD MAUNDER
Cambridge, 1988

MASS IN C MINOR

K 427

Edited by
Richard Maunder

W. A. MOZART
(1756–1791)

[1] Kyrie

OXFORD UNIVERSITY PRESS, MUSIC DEPARTMENT, WALTON STREET, OXFORD OX2 6DP

Mass in C Minor

Mass in C Minor

Mass in C Minor

Mass in C Minor

[2] Gloria in excelsis

Mass in C Minor

Mass in C Minor

Mass in C Minor

[3] Laudamus te

Mass in C Minor

Mass in C Minor

[4] Gratias agimus tibi

Mass in C Minor

[5] Domine Deus

Mass in C Minor

[6] Qui tollis

Mass in C Minor

Mass in C Minor

Mass in C Minor

Mass in C Minor

Mass in C Minor

Mass in C Minor

Mass in C Minor

Mass in C Minor

[7] Quoniam tu solus

Mass in C Minor

50

Mass in C Minor

Mass in C Minor

Mass in C Minor

Mass in C Minor

[8] Jesu Christe

[9] Cum Sancto Spiritu

Mass in C Minor

Mass in C Minor

Mass in C Minor

Mass in C Minor

[10] Credo in unum Deum

Mass in C Minor

Mass in C Minor

Mass in C Minor

[11] Et incarnatus est

Andante ma sostenuto

SOPRANO
SOLO

Et in - car - na - tus est

Mass in C Minor

Mass in C Minor

tus est.

Mass in C Minor

[12] Sanctus

Mass in C Minor

Mass in C Minor

33

in — ex - cel — — —

O – san-na in ex – cel-sis. O – san – — —

– san – na, o – san – na in — ex – cel – sis. O – san – na,

o – san – na in — ex – cel — — — — sis. O – san – na, o –

— — — — — — — — sis, — — — — — — — — na, o – san-na, o – san — —

— — na in ex — cel – sis, in ex – cel – sis, in ex – cel-sis. O – san – na,

O-san – na, o – san – na,

39

Mass in C Minor

106

Mass in C Minor

57

-san - na in ex - cel - sis, in ex - cel - sis. O - san - na in ex -

-san - na in ex - cel - sis, in ex - cel - sis. O - san - na in ex -

-san - na in ex - cel - sis, in ex - cel - sis. O - san - na in ex -

-san - na in ex - cel - sis, in ex - cel - sis. O - san - na in ex -

O - san - na in ex - cel - sis. O - san - na in ex - cel - sis,

O - san - na in ex - cel - sis. O - san - na in ex - cel - sis,

O - san - na in ex - cel - sis. O - san - na in ex - cel - sis,

O - san - na in ex - cel - sis. O - san - na in ex - cel - sis,

Mass in C Minor

[13] Benedictus

Mass in C Minor

Mass in C Minor

114

Mass in C Minor

Mass in C Minor

Mass in C Minor

Mass in C Minor

Mass in C Minor

Mass in C Minor

116

in ex - cel - sis. O - san - na in ex - cel - sis, in ex - cel - sis.

in ex - cel - sis. O - san - na in ex - cel - sis, in ex - cel - sis.

in ex - cel - sis. O - san - na in ex - cel - sis, in ex - cel - sis.

in ex - cel - sis. O - san - na in ex - cel - sis, in ex - cel - sis.

in ex - cel - sis. O - san - na in ex - cel - sis. O -

in ex - cel - sis. O - san - na in ex - cel - sis. O -

in ex - cel - sis. O - san - na in ex - cel - sis. O -

in ex - cel - sis. O - san - na in ex - cel - sis. O -

Mass in C Minor

Processed and printed by
Halstan & Co. Ltd., Amersham, Bucks., England